Dr. Nakeisha Mahar

Email: nakeisha25@yahoo.com

Copyright © 2021 July by Dr. Nakeisha Maharaj

All rights reserved.

No part of this publication may be reproduced, stored in a retrieval system or transmitted in any form or by any means; electronic photocopying, recording or otherwise without prior authorization of the author, Dr Nakeisha Maharaj.

Printed in USA

ISBN: 978-1-7367197-4-9

Library of Congress Control Number: 2021912888

I dedicate this book to every child. Know that God loves you, and He is only a conversation away.

There is so much I am thankful for that I had to come back and say.

My day was filled with lots of fun.

Today, when I got upset and my thoughts wanted to stray,

Thank you, God, for not calling my family to Heaven.

I'm not ready to lose my mom, dad, or little sister, who recently turned seven.

That's why today I helped the little boy who was crying because he couldn't tie his favorite shoe.

Thank you, God, for not allowing our food basket to run dry.

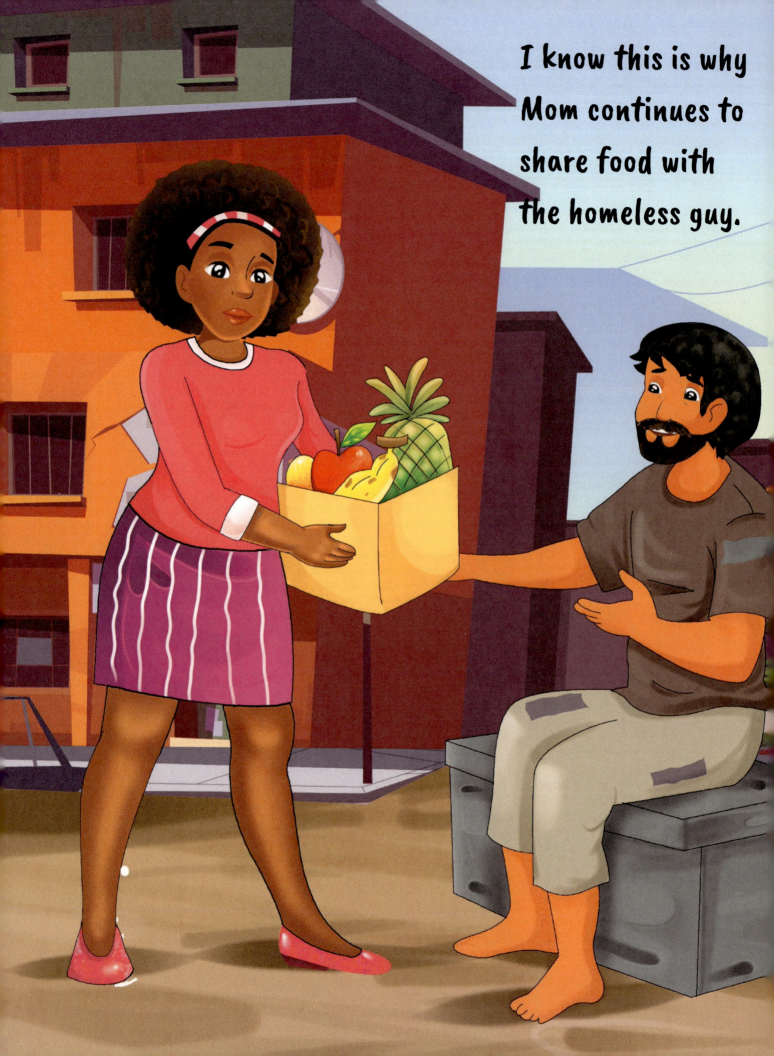

As I look back on my day, I realize there are so many blessings I could thank you for today.

7-Scriptural

Affirmation - Amplified Bible

I am a gift from the Lord.

—Psalm 127:3

Behold, children are a heritage and gift

from the Lord,

The fruit of the womb a reward.

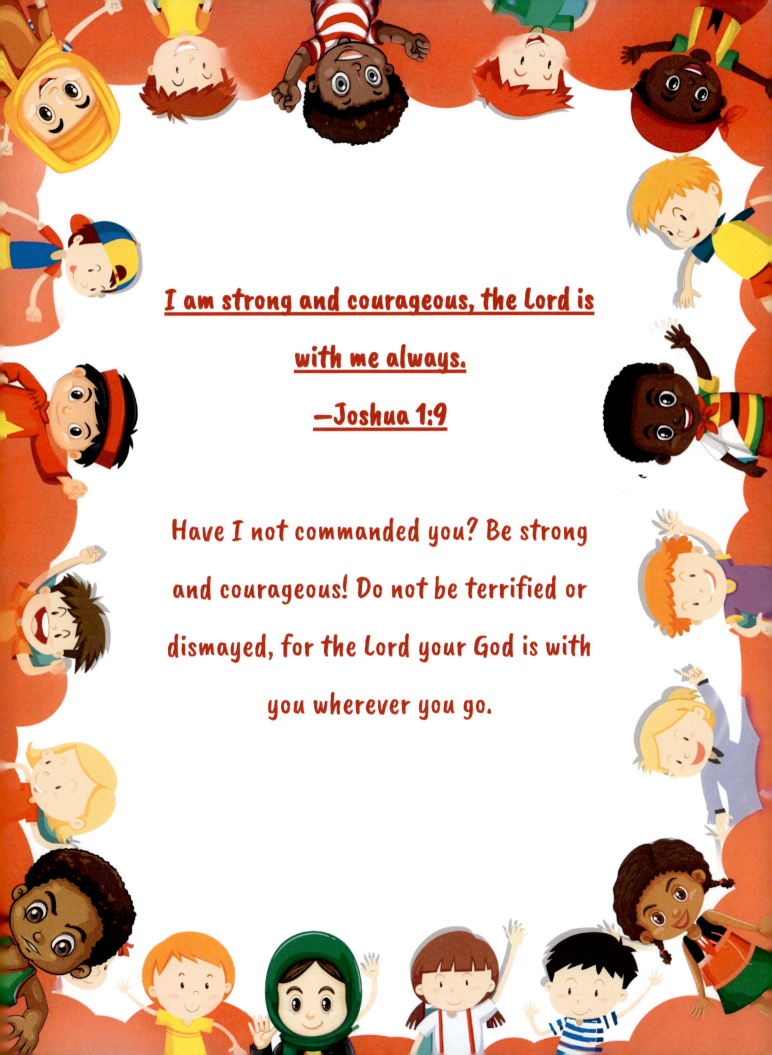

I am strong and courageous, the Lord is with me always.

—Joshua 1:9

Have I not commanded you? Be strong and courageous! Do not be terrified or dismayed, for the Lord your God is with you wherever you go.

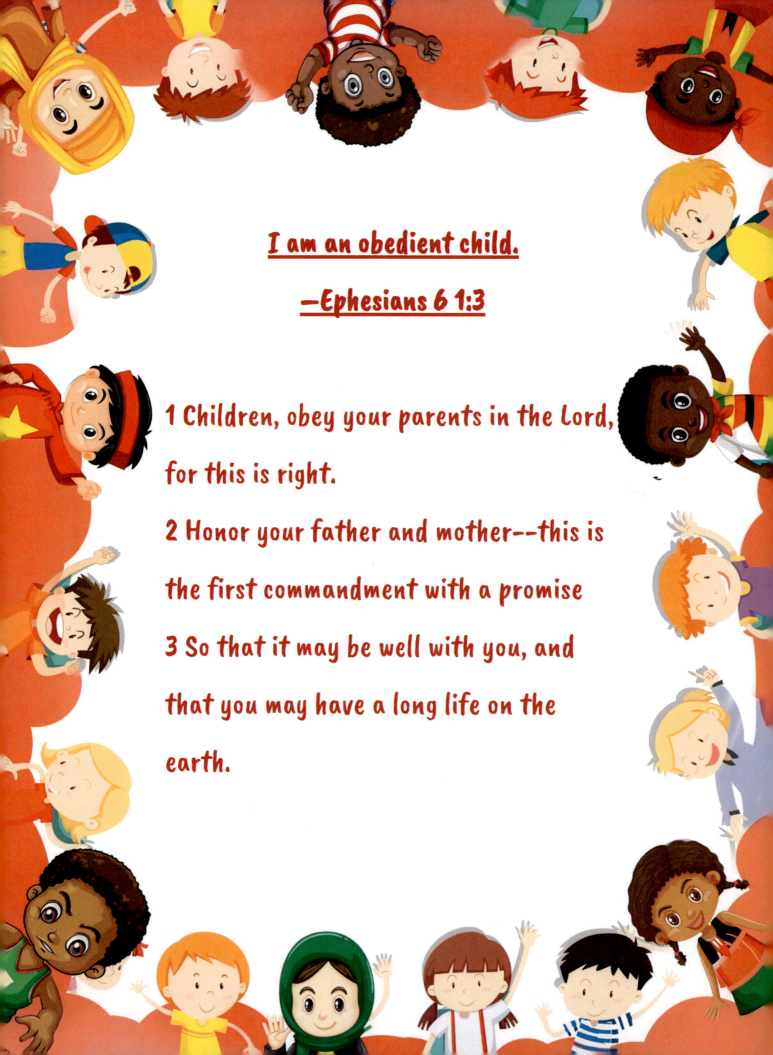

I am an obedient child.
—Ephesians 6 1:3

1 Children, obey your parents in the Lord, for this is right.

2 Honor your father and mother--this is the first commandment with a promise

3 So that it may be well with you, and that you may have a long life on the earth.

I am loved by God.

−1 John 4:19

We love, because He first loved us.

<u>I can do anything I set my mind to.</u>

<u>—Philippians 4:13</u>

I can do all things through Him who strengthens and empowers me.

I am never alone or afraid.

—Deuteronomy 31-8

It is the Lord who goes before you;

He will be with you.

He will not fail you or abandon you.

Do not fear or be dismayed.

<u>*I have everything I need.*</u>

<u>*—Psalm 23:1*</u>

The Lord is my Shepherd, I shall not want.

What are five things you are thankful for today?

1. _____

2. _____

3. _____

4. _____

5. _____

Just as the mom in this book gave food to the homeless man or the boy helped tie another boy's shoe, who have you helped today?

1. _____

_____

2. _____

_____

3. _____

_____

Praying is simply talking to God as you would talk to a friend. Is there someone or something you would like to talk to God about?

1. _____

_____

2. _____

_____

3. _____

_____

A Special Prayer for You

Father God, I thank you for your grace and your mercy. I pray now that you bless the person reading or listening to this book right now. May your divine hands always be upon them. Increase their wisdom, knowledge, and understanding. May your purpose be fulfilled in their life, and may they walk in increase and blessings now and forevermore. I pray for every child to know and feel loved by you, Father God. Guide and protect them always. Let your angels watch over them wherever they go. Help them to make wise decisions daily and teach them how to be a blessing to others. I pray they will always count their blessings in every situation—even when it seems like there are none. Amen!!

Thank you for taking the time to read this book today, I hope you enjoyed it as much as I enjoyed writing it.

I would love to share your feedback with my kids so be sure to click the 5 ✺ rating on Amazon and Goodreads and leave us a great review.

With an adult permission, feel free to send us a photo of you and one of our books at NAKEISHA25@YAHOO.COM to win a special prize.

Check out more books of Dr Nakeisha below.

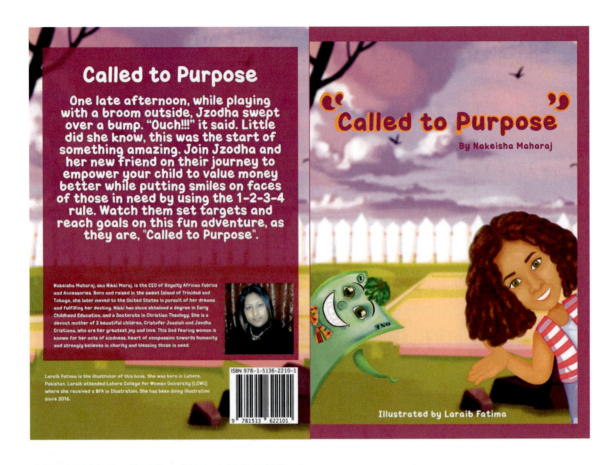

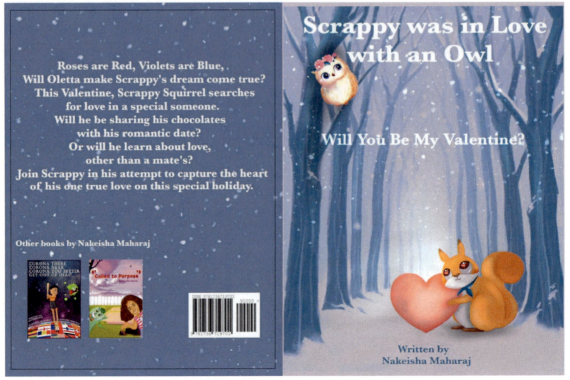

Made in the USA
Middletown, DE
03 April 2022